This Coloring Book Belongs To:

_____

Cheers for purschasing My Stoner Coloring Book!

I'm glad that you chose to spend some time coloring and relaxing with this fun coloring book.
I hope that you will have a wonderful time.

Thank you,

Joint Jo

Copyright 2021 Joint Jo Books

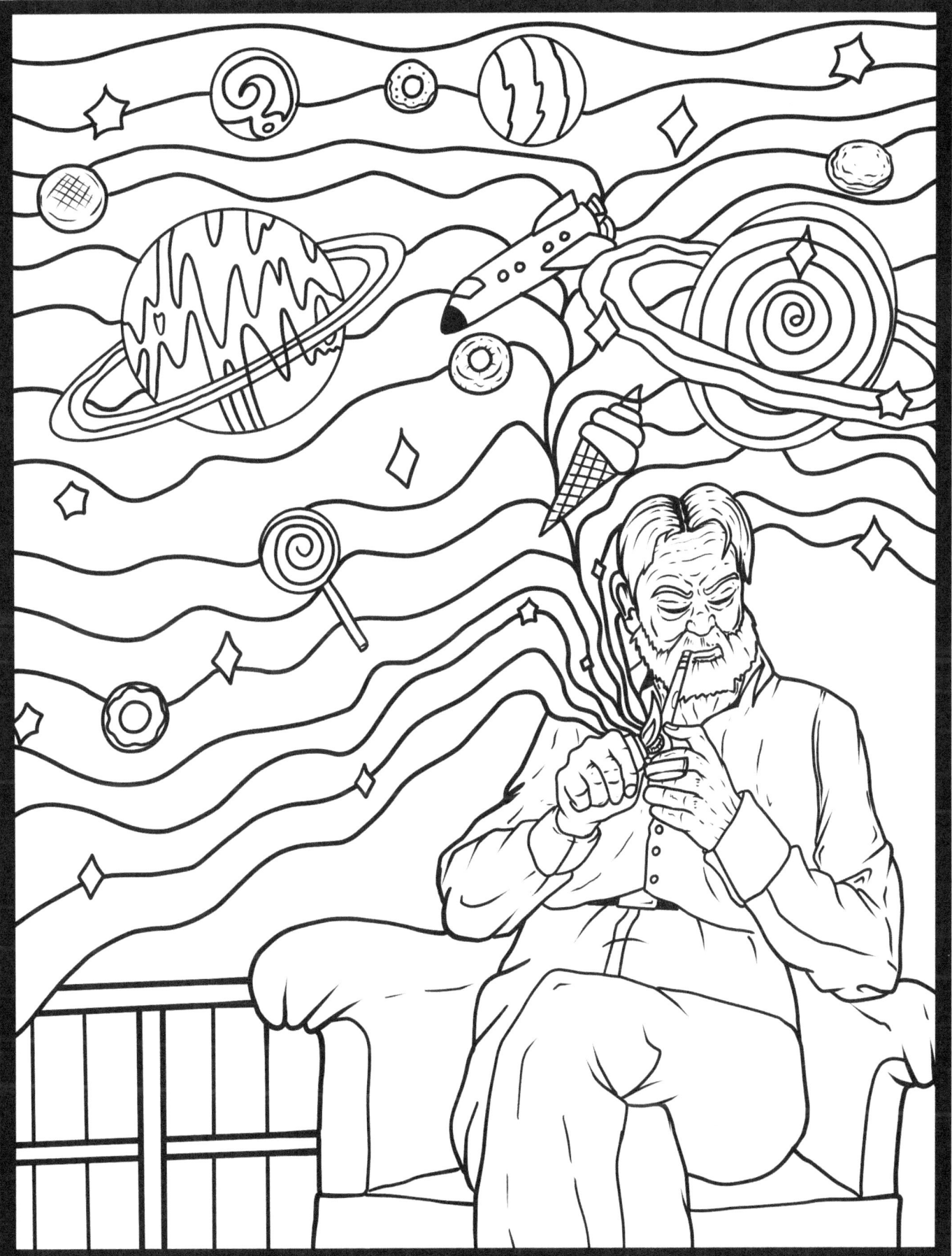

after work sesh

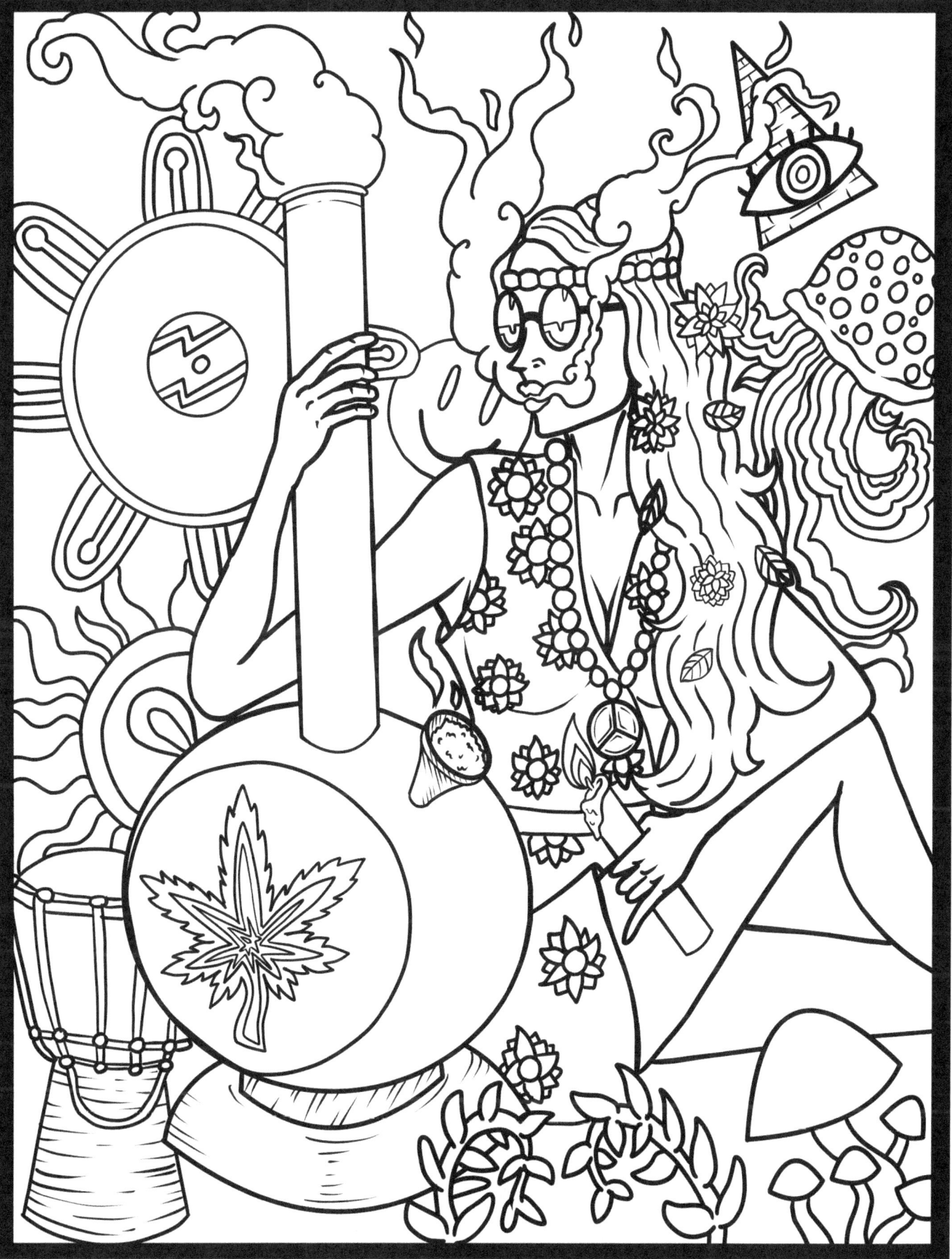

Lady hippy

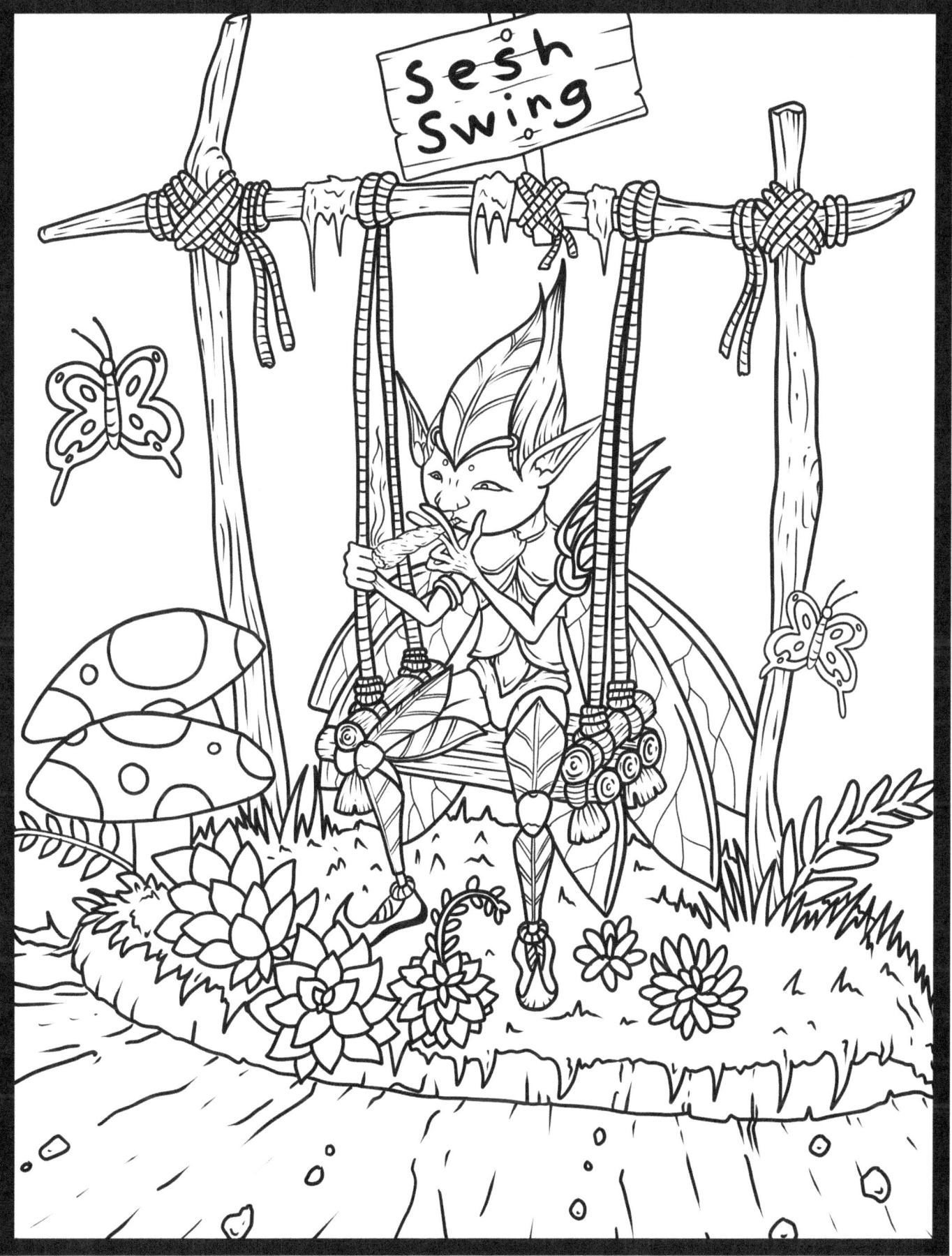

Fairy stoner

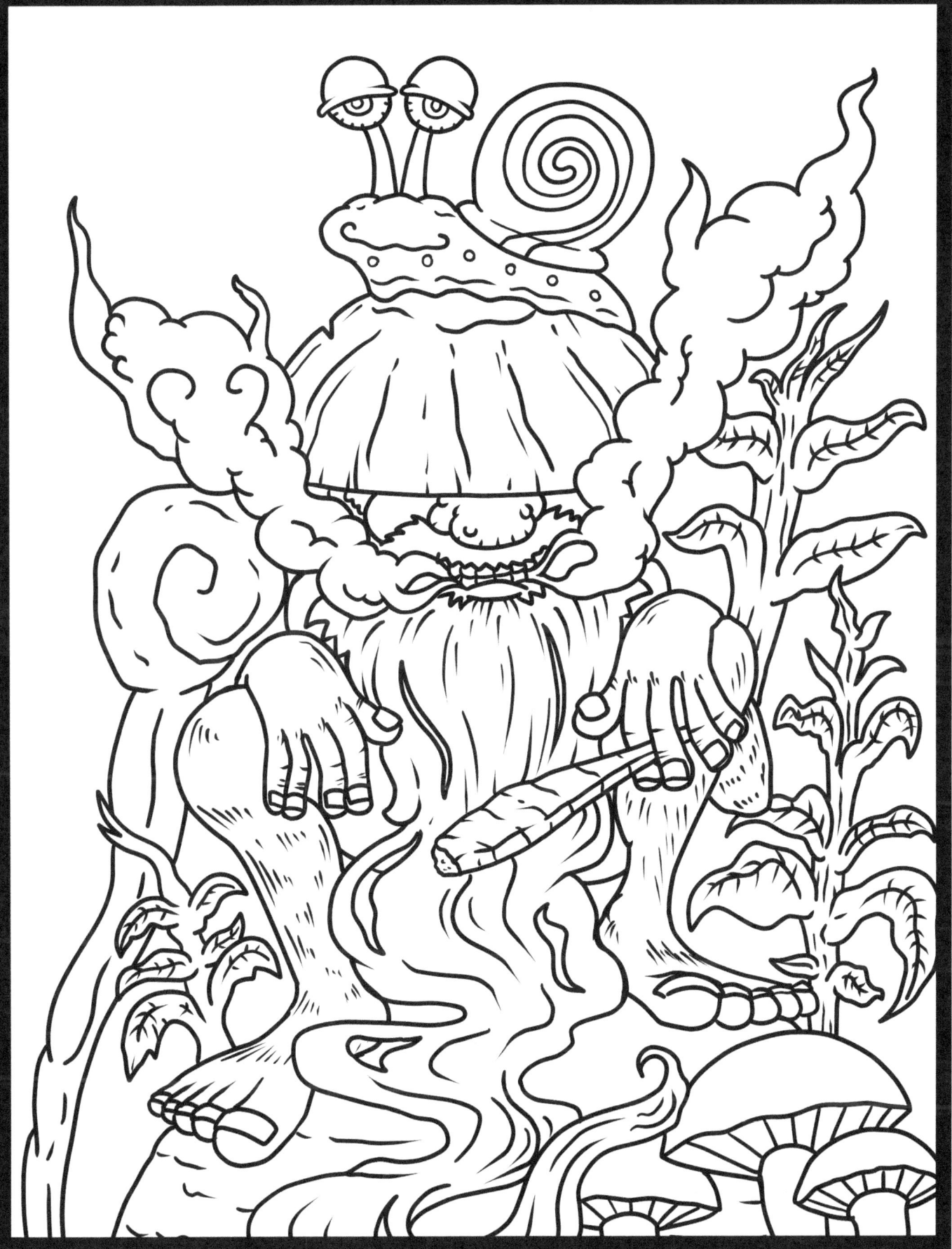

chillin with my snail

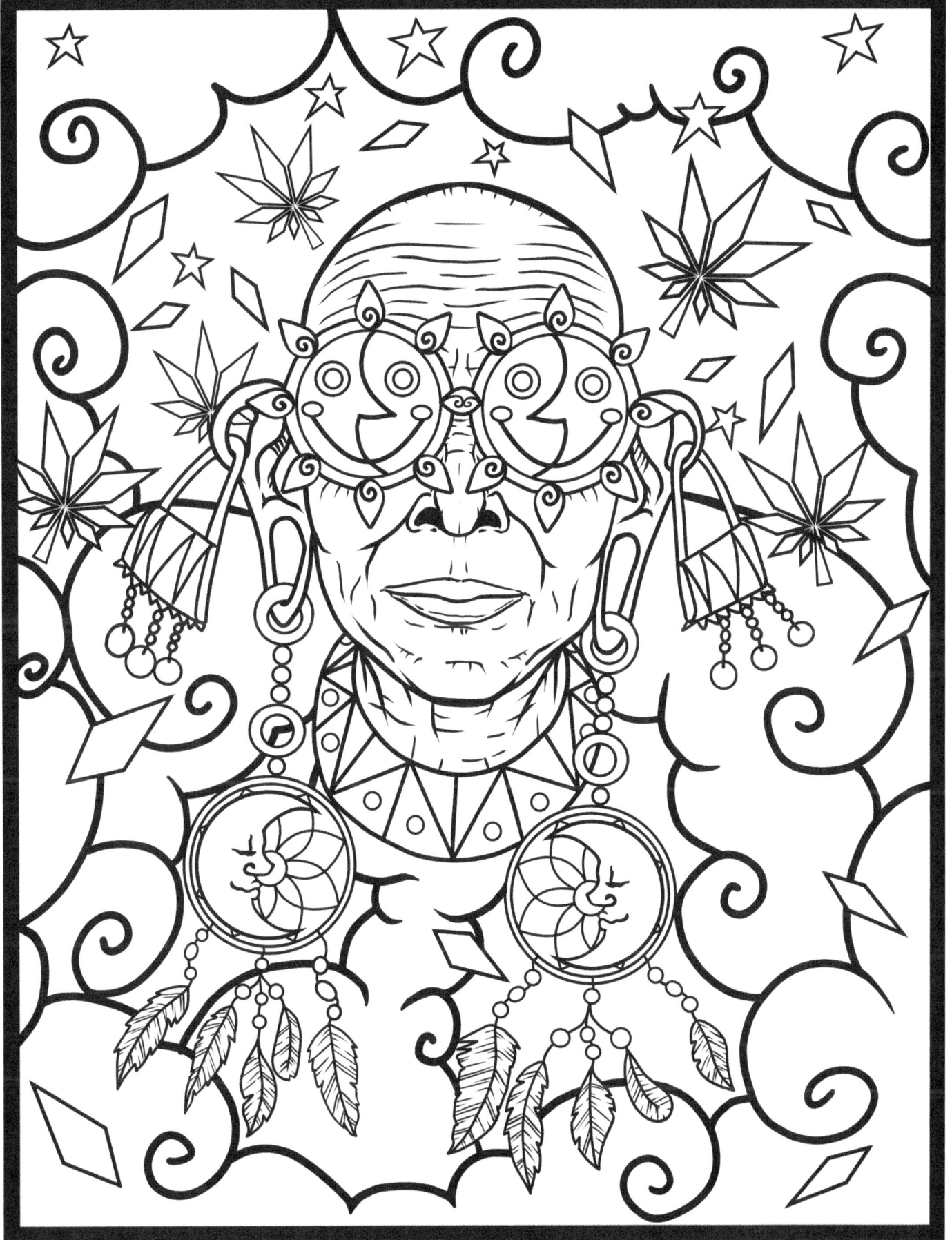

Dreamscape

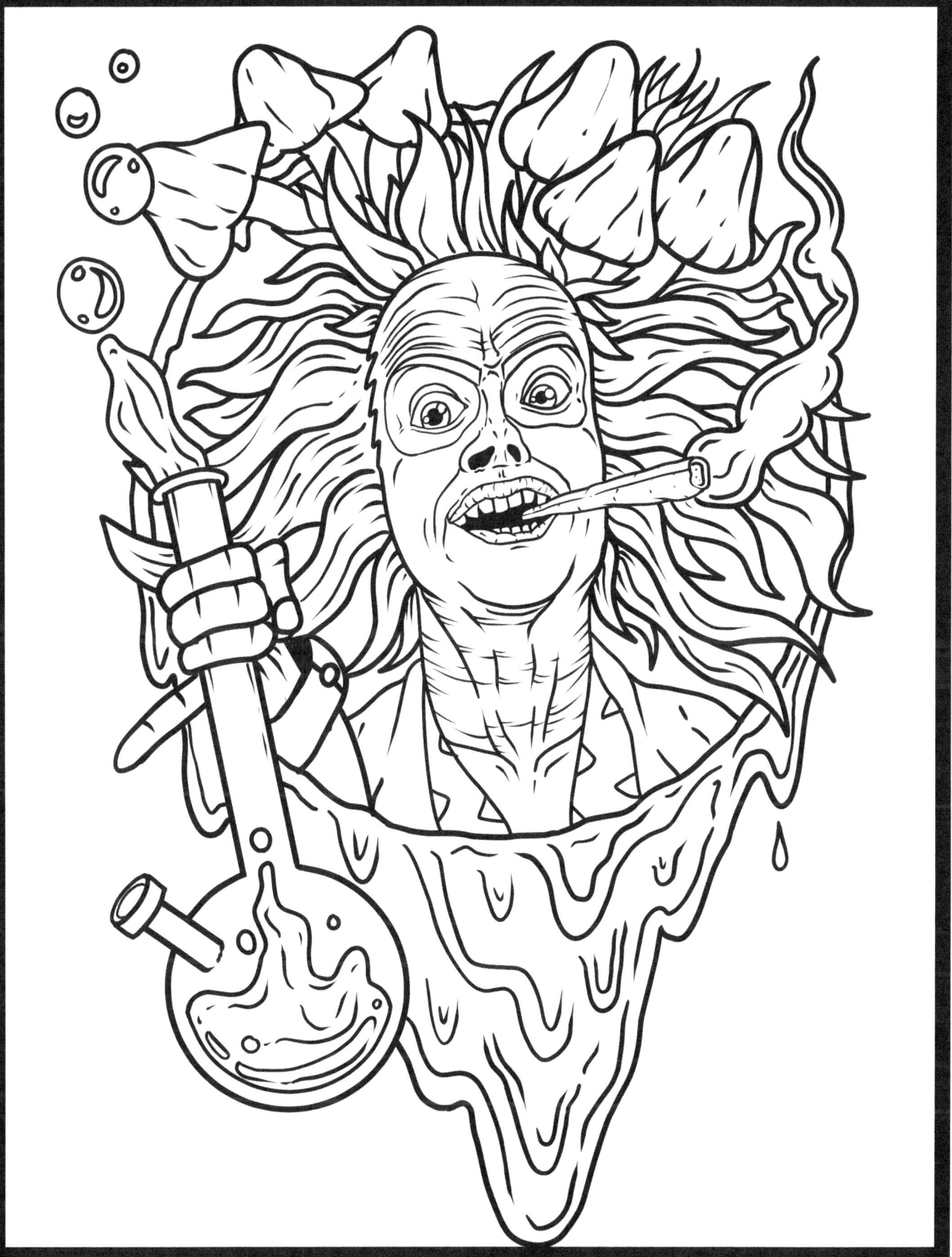

Melt with me

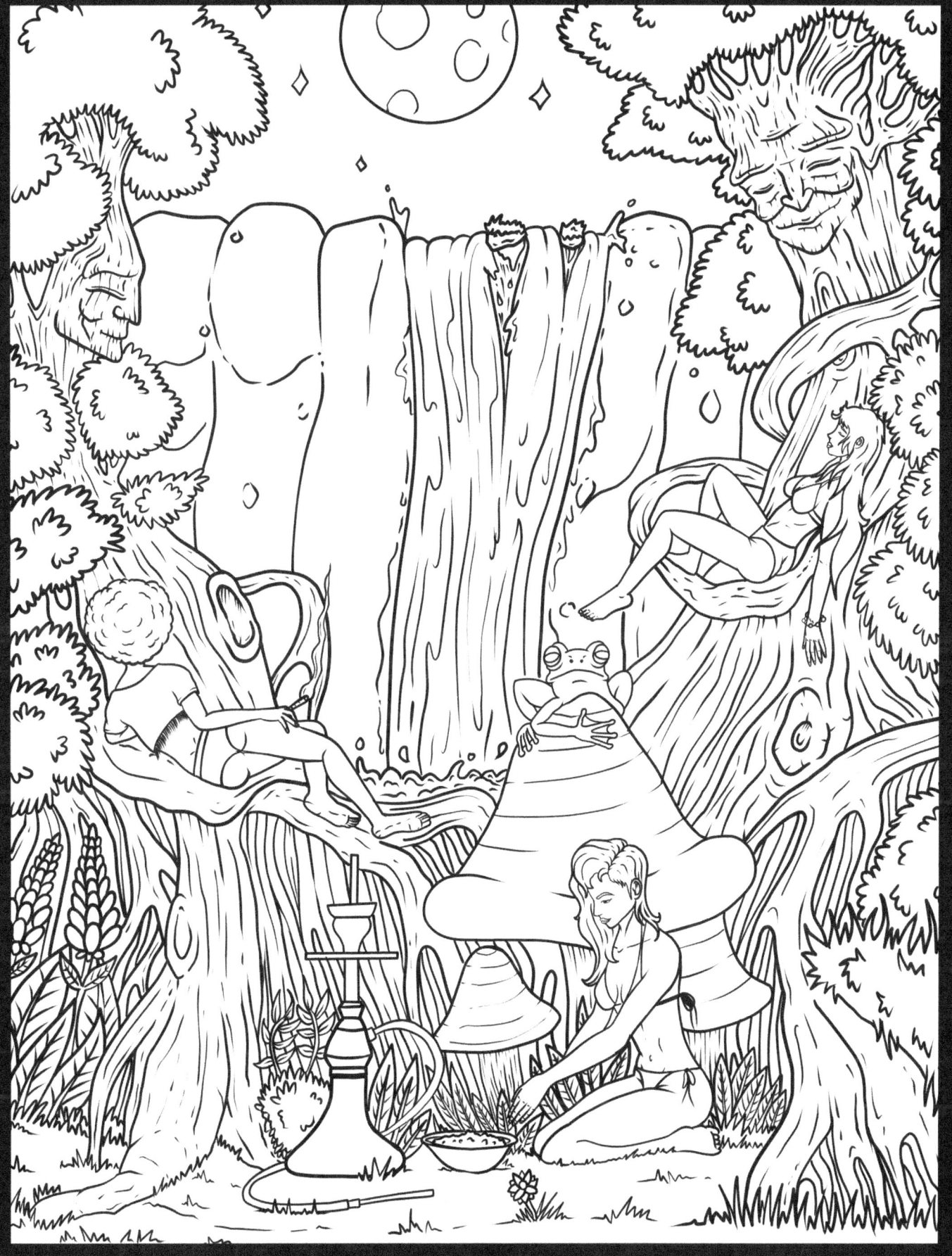

Chill Forest

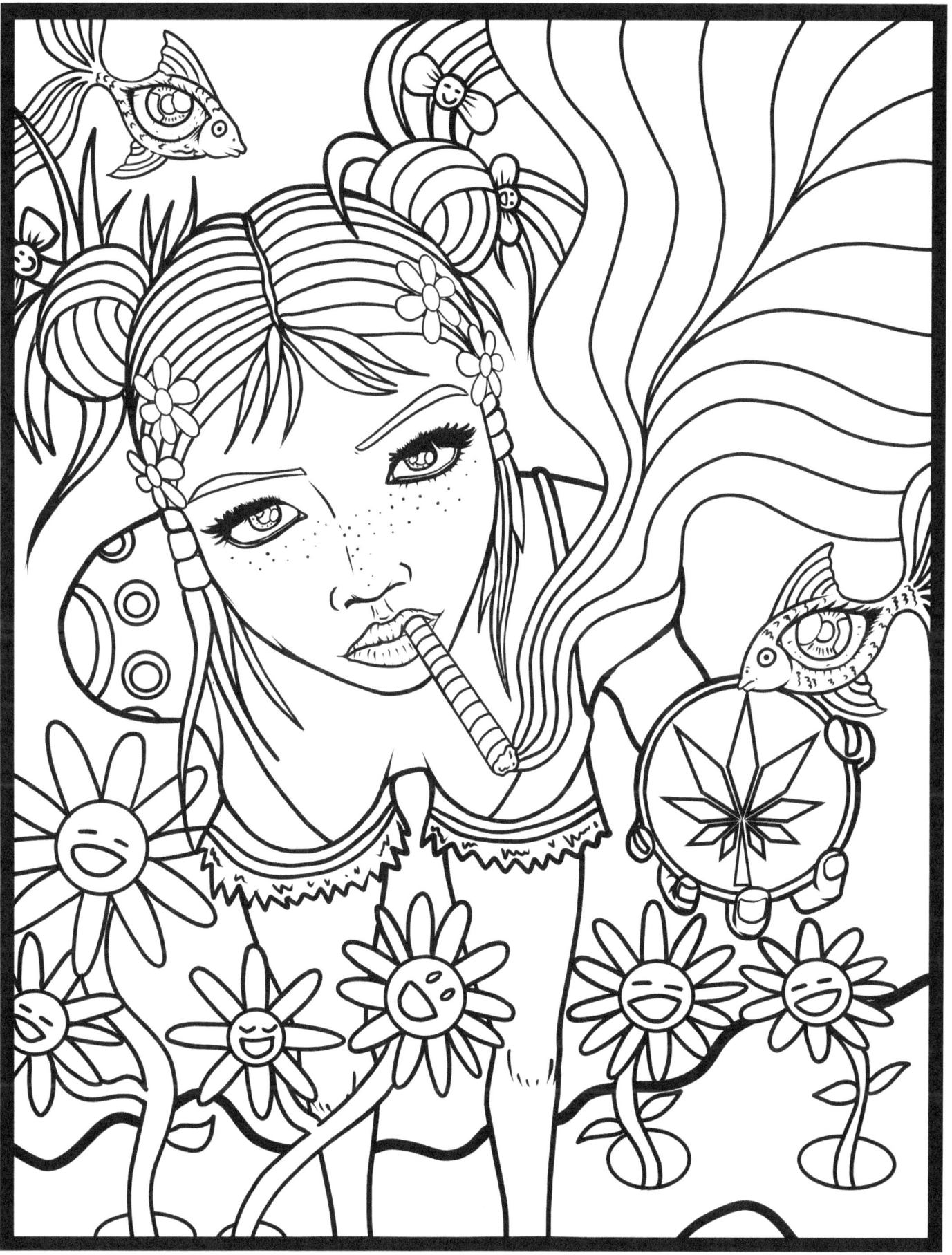

S.W.A.

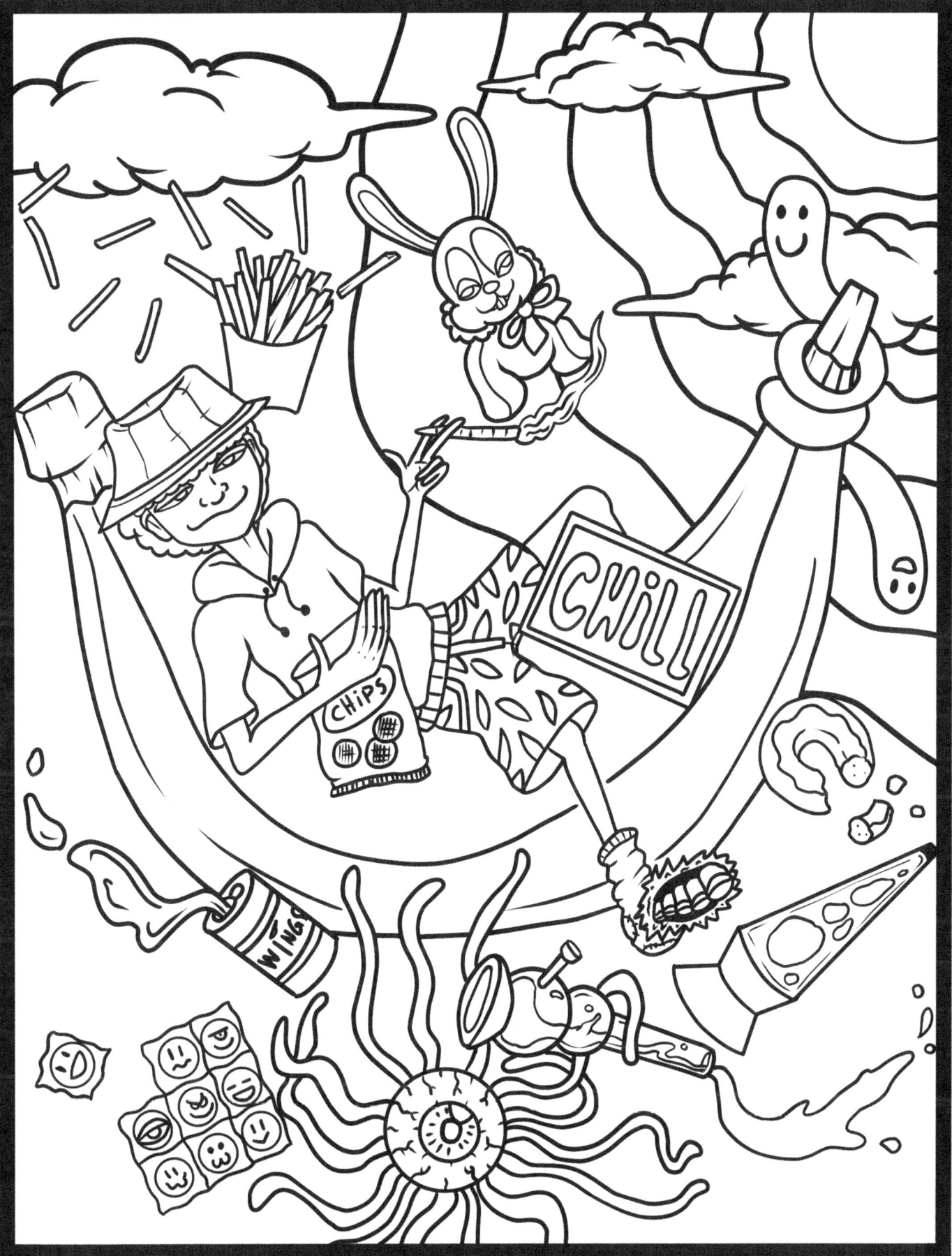

Trippin' N Chillin'

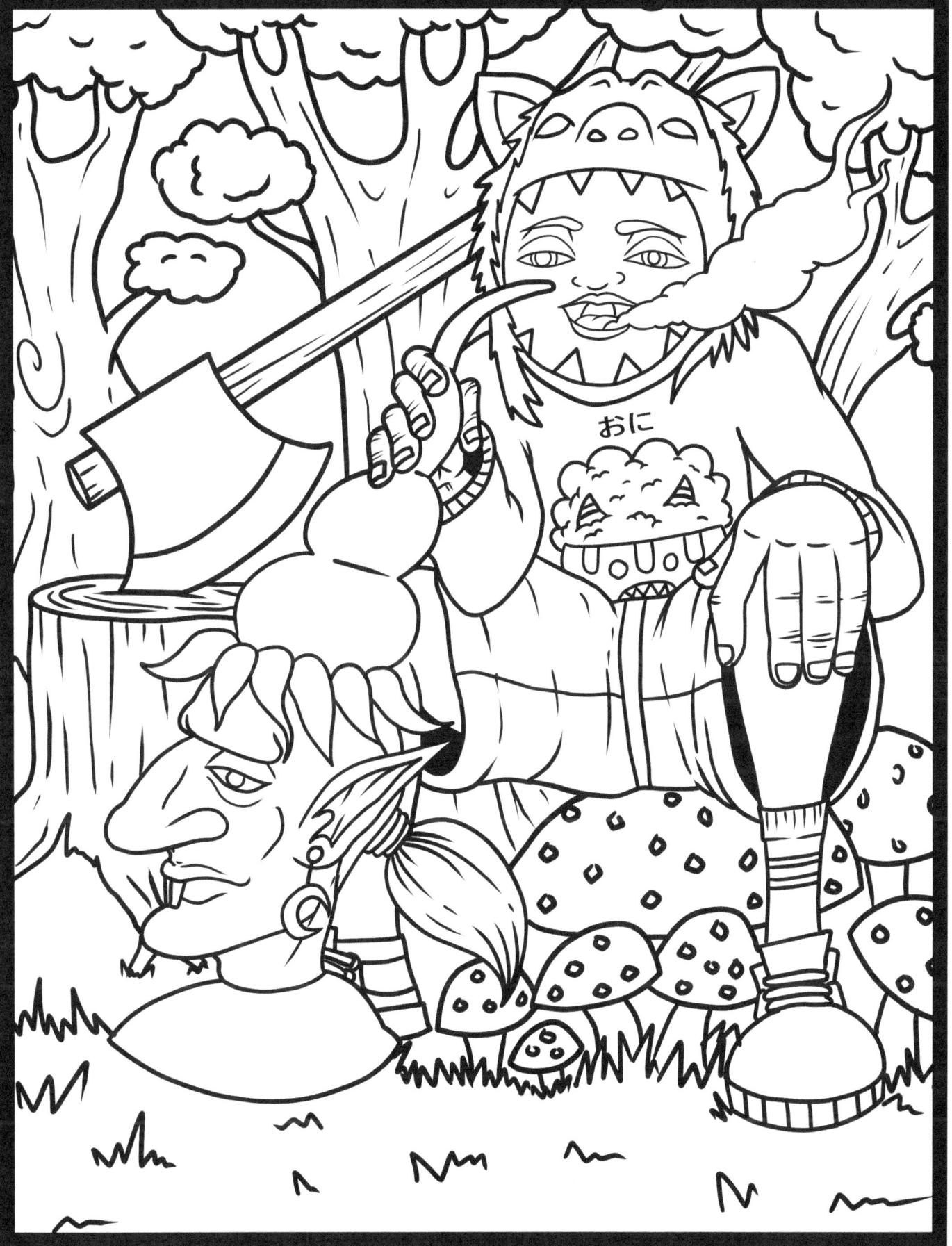

Lumber 420

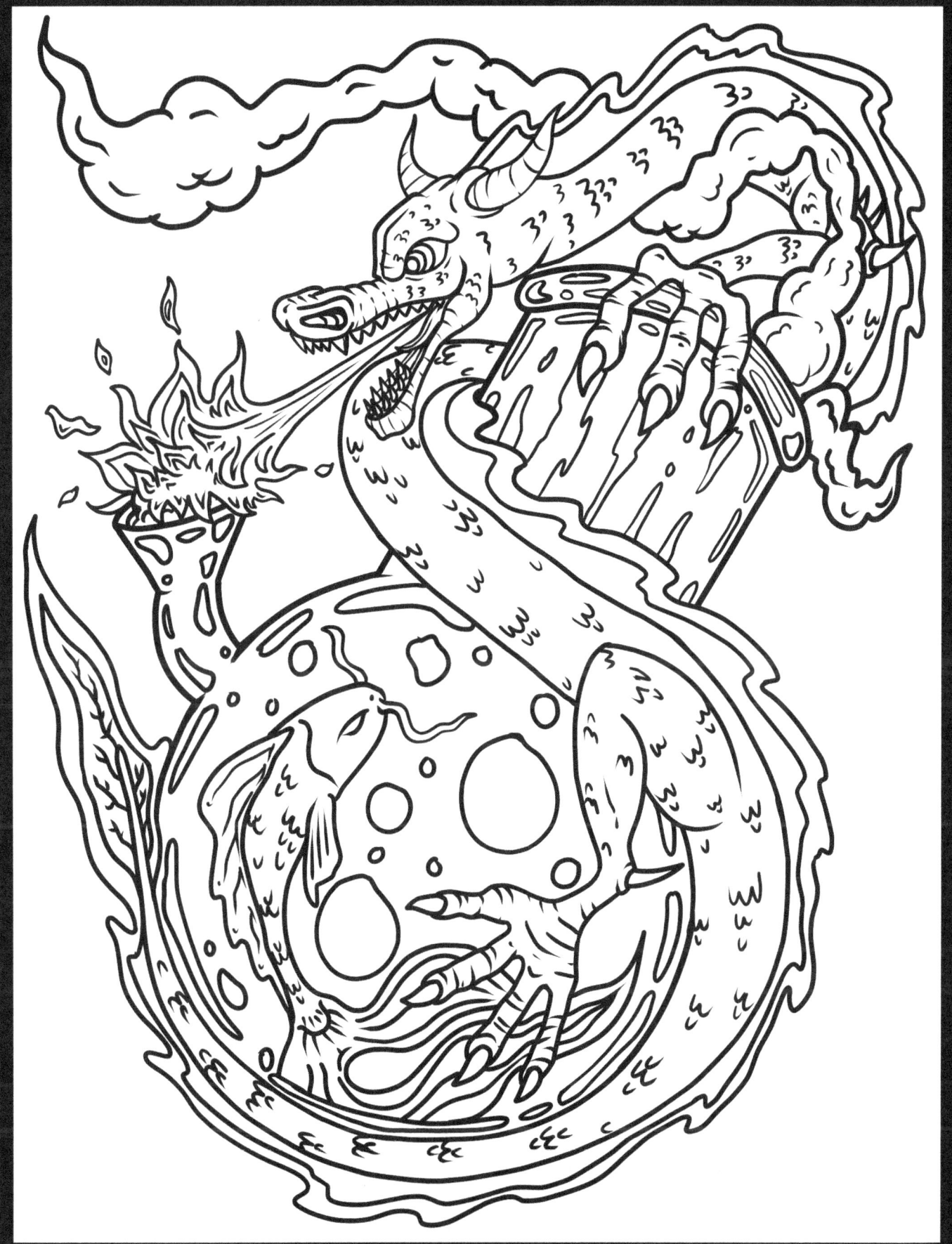

Puff of Asia

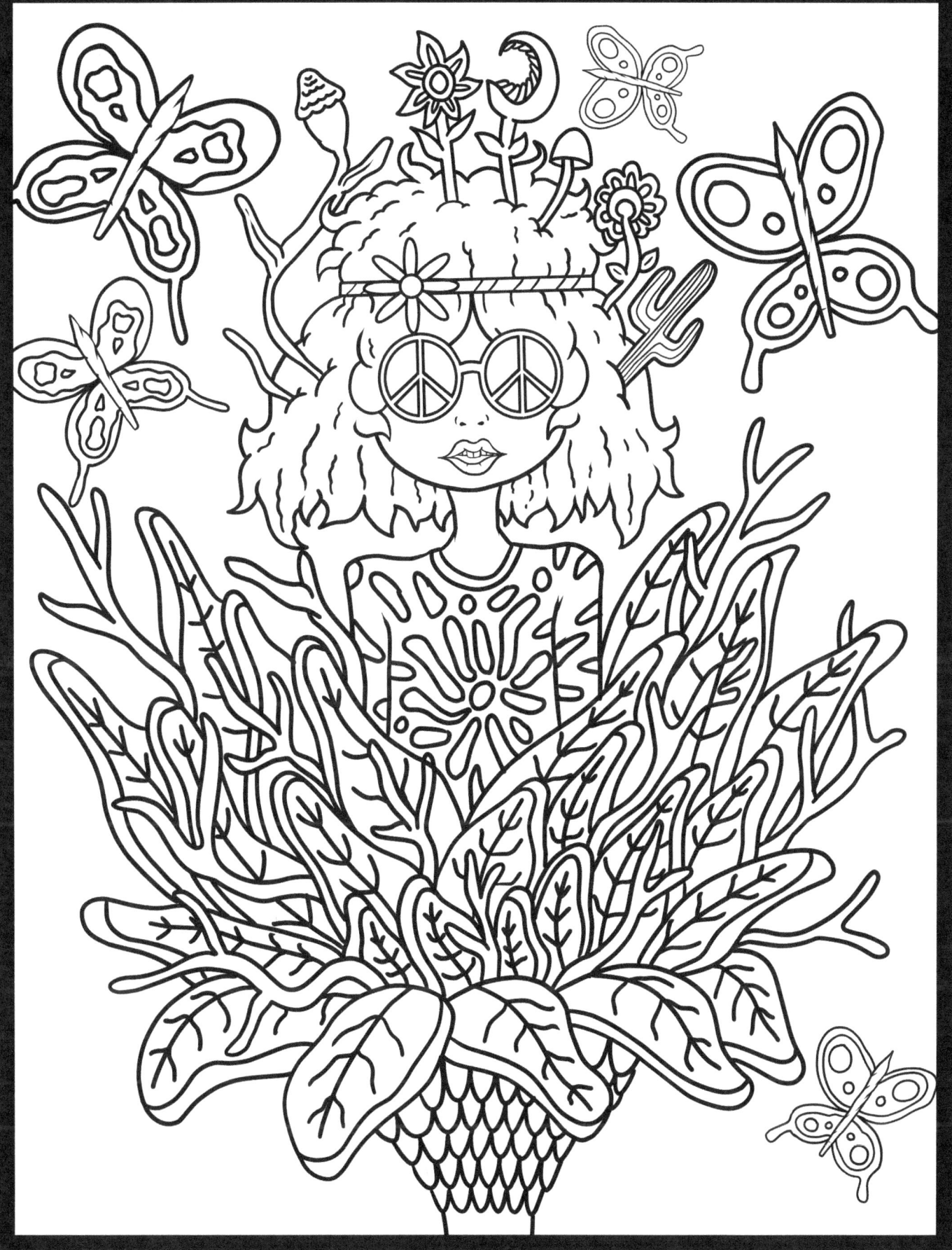

Sweet Buds

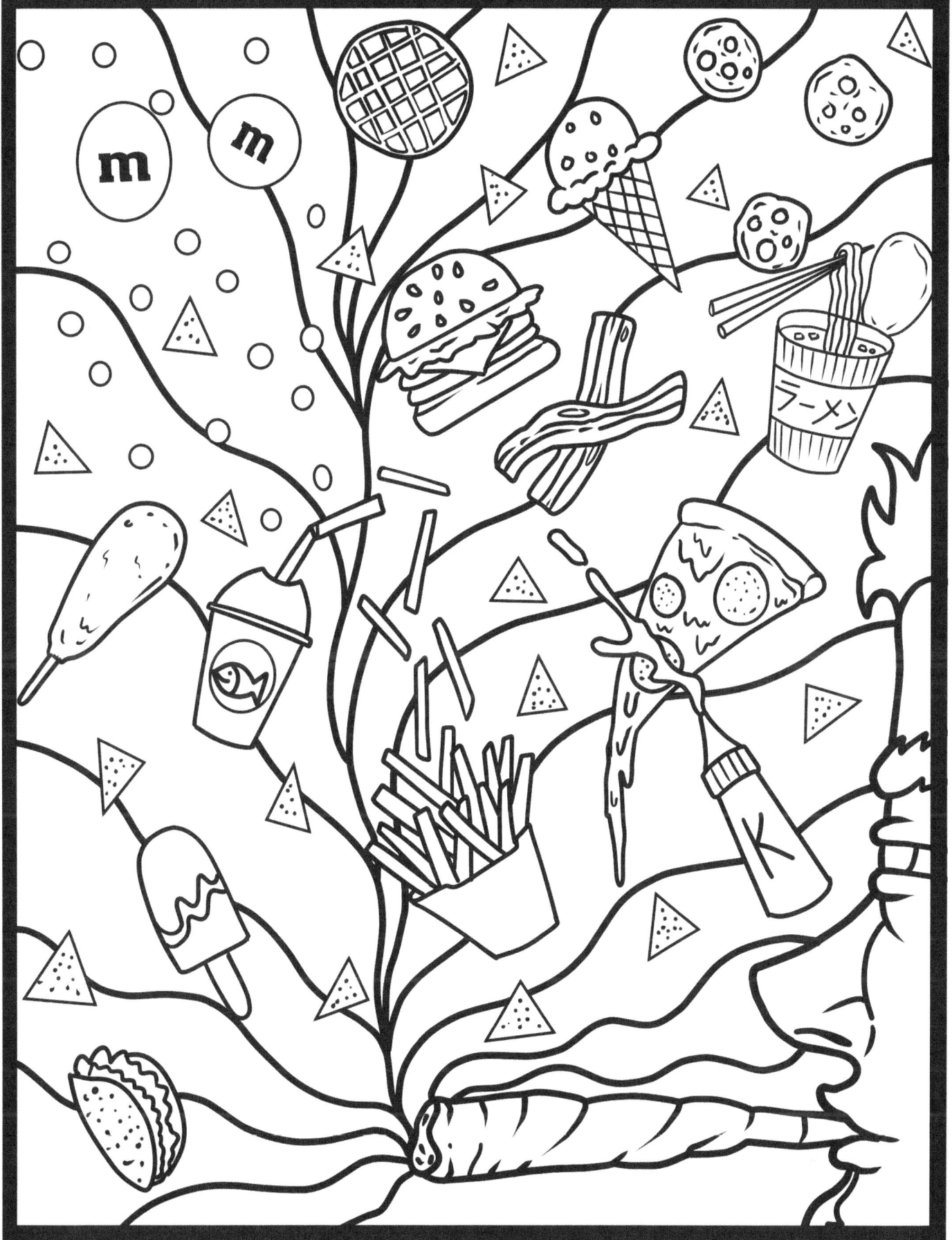

Munchies in my mind

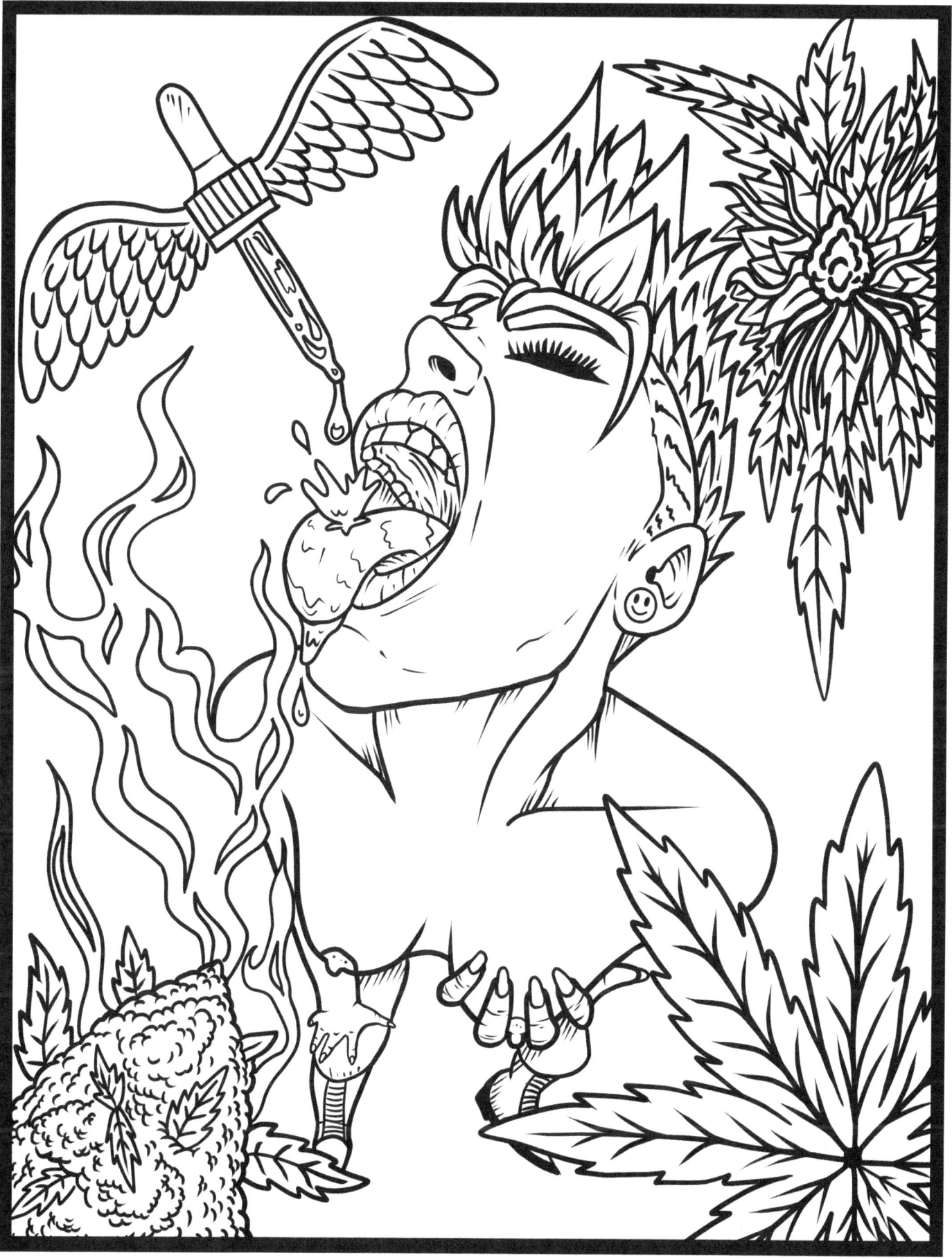

ACID N WEED

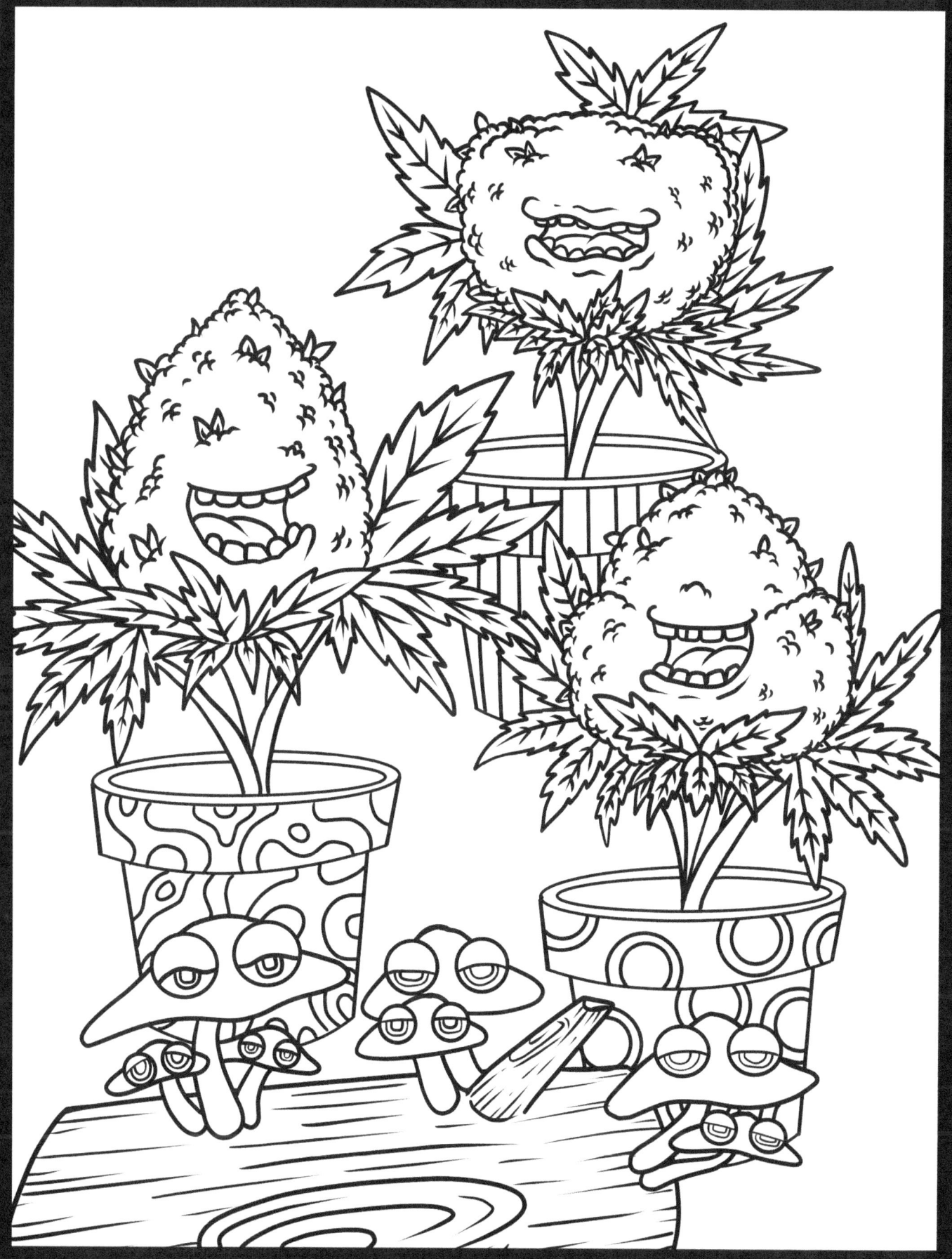

Happy Buds

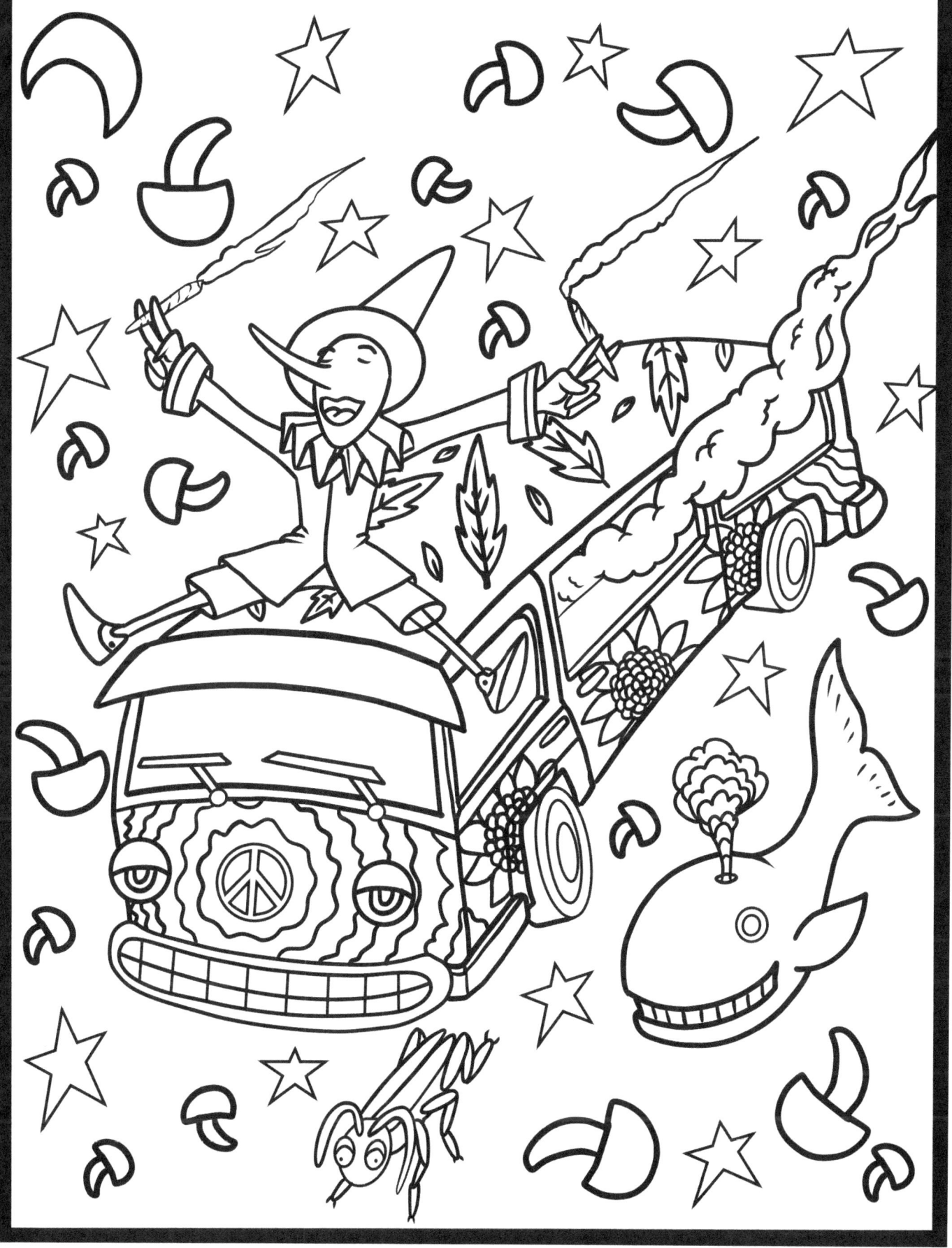

Pinnochio's Trippy Bus

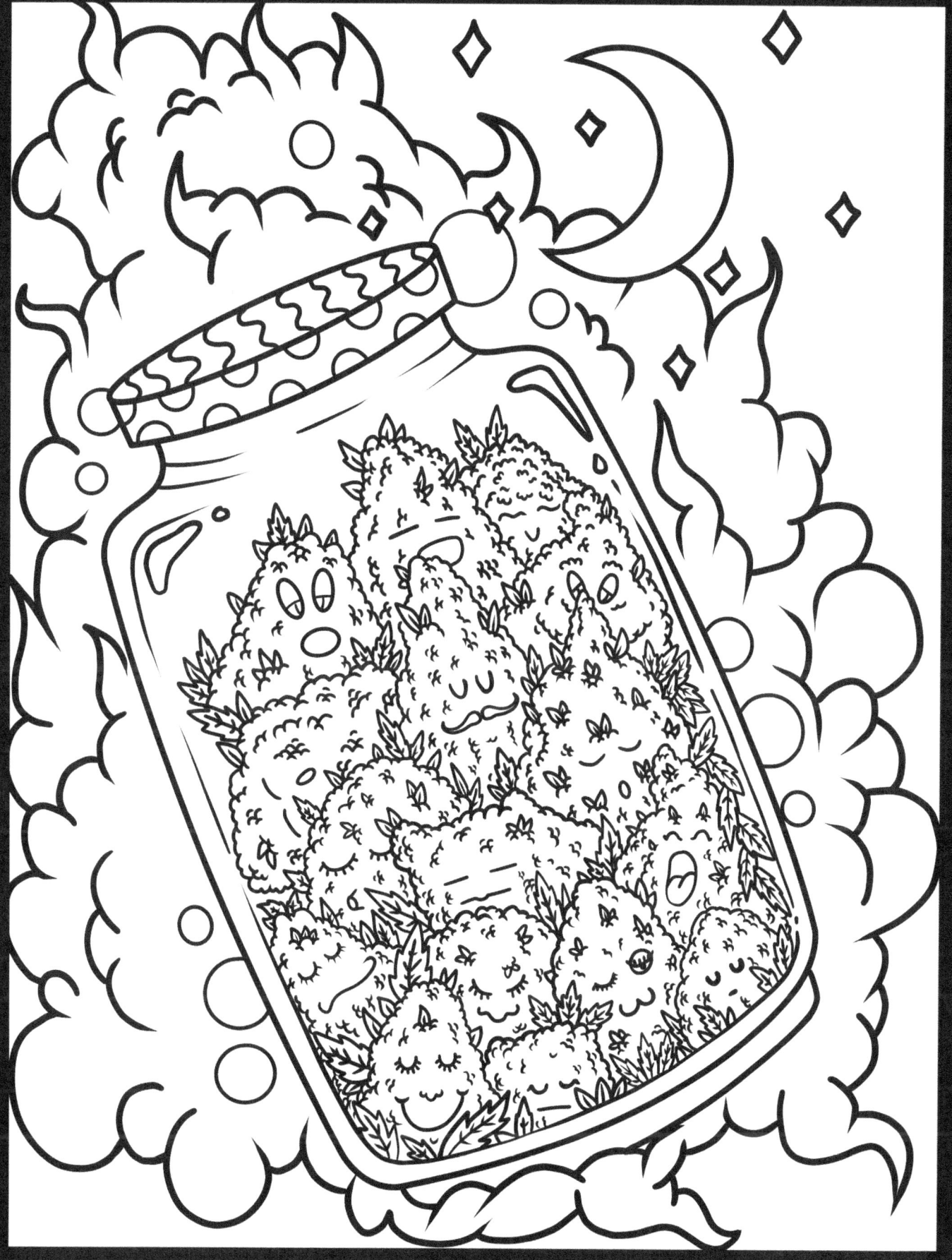

The Stash

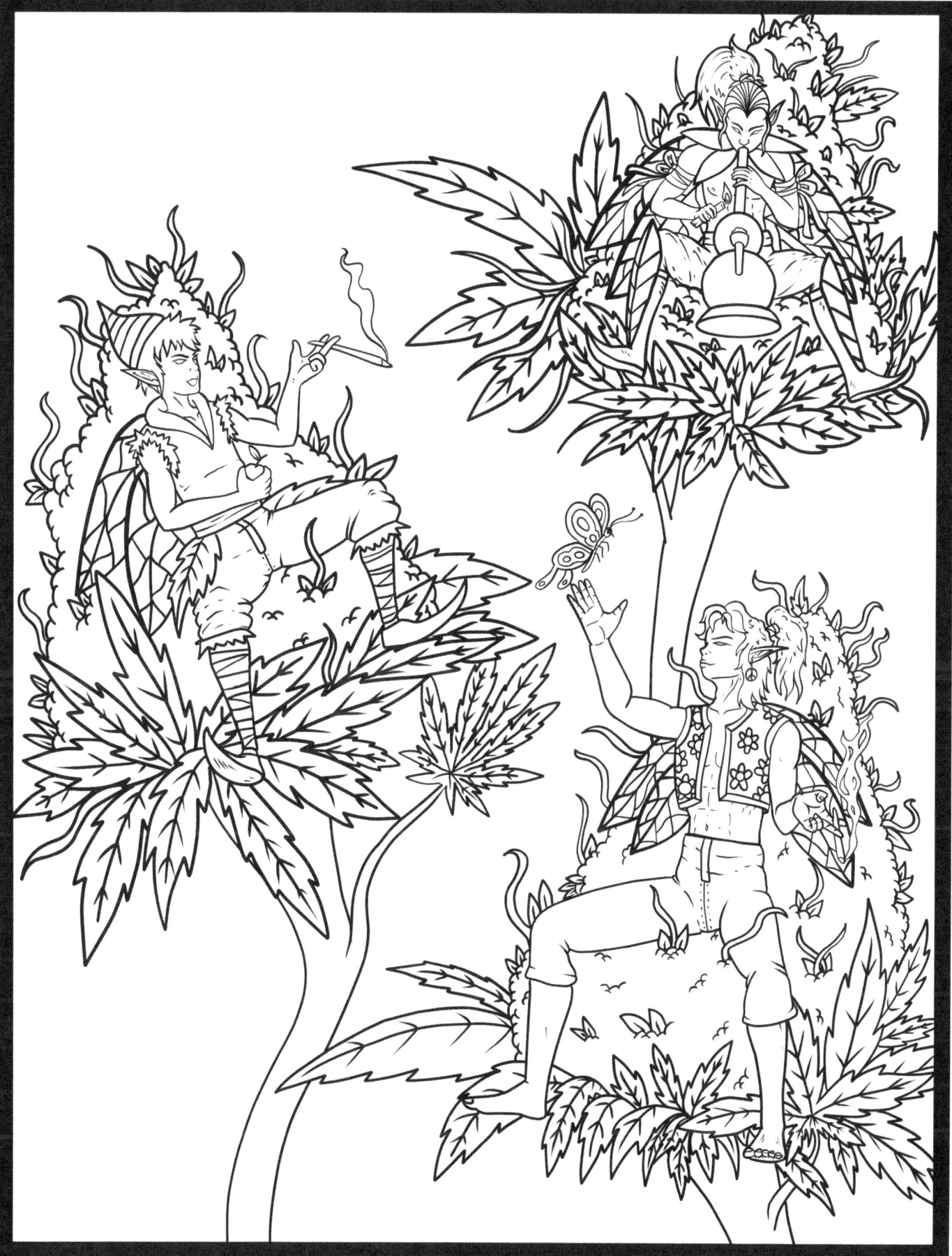

Chillin' with the boys

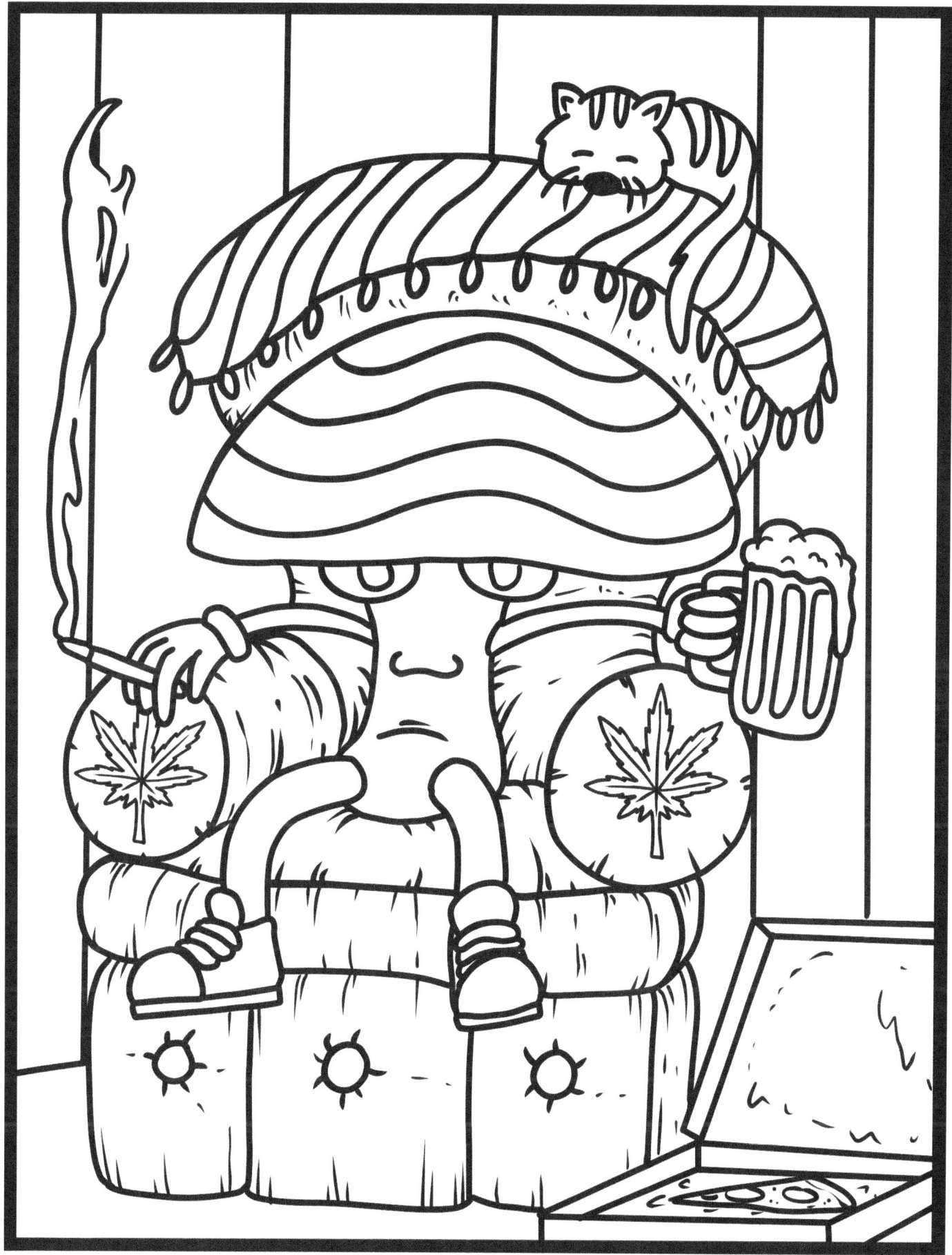

Mushroom Fridays

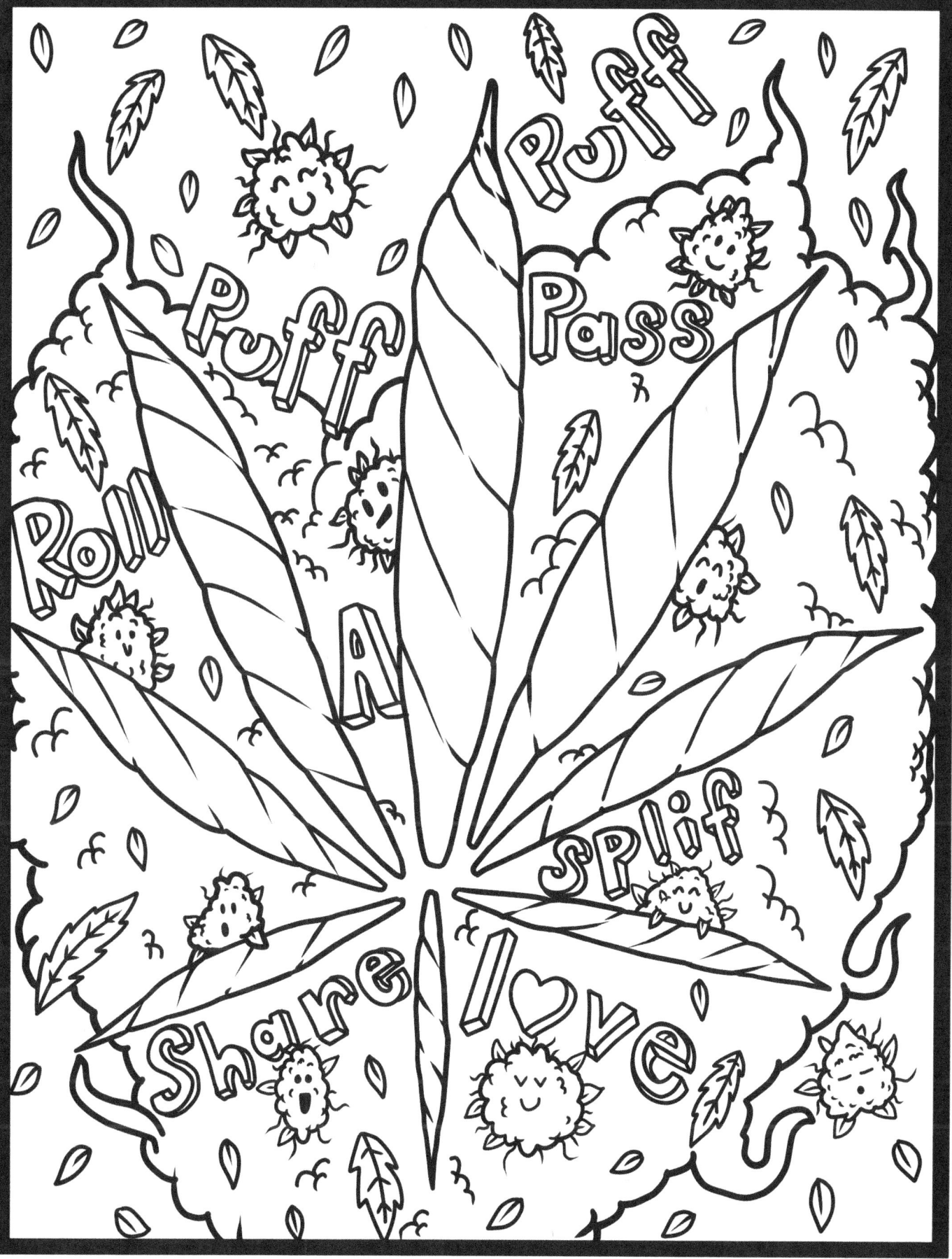

Splifs of love

www.ingramcontent.com/pod-product-compliance
Lightning Source LLC
Chambersburg PA
CBHW081059240526
45465CB00025B/2772